HEAVENLY GLASSES: VISION CHECK

2nd Edition

Ebony Collins

EBONY COLLINS

Copyright © 2022 Ebony Collins

All rights reserved.

ISBN-13: **979-8-9851343-1-5**

DEDICATION

I dedicate this book to my children: Bryanna, Christian, Skylar, Seven, and Genesis Collins. The five of you are my heartbeat. You push me to be better, try harder, and believe more. You inspire me to give my all in every situation that I encounter. You believe in me, trust me, and you love me regardless of what I do. I pray that someday when you feel discouraged, you can pick up this book and read Mommy's words. Know that they were inspired by God and feel your help. I pray that you live life wearing your heavenly glasses, always seeing God even if you can't find the good. Thank you for your love. I will forever love you.

CONTENTS

	Acknowledgments	i
1	Faith	**1**
2	GPS	**15**
3	Pride	**21**
4	Let Go	**29**
5	Judas	**39**
6	Unexpected Hardships	**45**
7	Forgiveness	**53**
8	Dream Killers	**63**
9	Delay Not Denial	**71**
10	Favor Ain't Fair	**79**
11	Cracks in Your Circle	**89**
12	Entertaining Angels	**97**
13	The Book of Job	**103**
14	Dear Children	**111**

ACKNOWLEDGMENTS

First, giving honor to my Lord and Savior Jesus Christ. I thank you for your grace and mercy that covers me all the days of my life. I thank you for the strength during this journey of enlightenment. I thank you for the peace that covers me in moments of turmoil.

To my wonderful, supportive, and loving husband, Bryan, I love you. You push, encourage, support, uplift, and inspire me. I thank you for everything you have contributed to my life, to my dreams, and my heart these past few years. You are my friend and I value you so much.

To my parents, Pamela and Martin Ragin Sr. Thank you for always telling me that I could be and do anything that I set my mind to. You never allow me to quit or speak negatively about myself. Because of your sacrifices in life, I am who I am. I only pray that I continue to make you proud to call me daughter.

Anyone who knows me knows that my siblings are my babies. Martin Jr., Maleeka, Romaine, Destiny, Nicole, Keiyonna, Shawnya, Savoy, Jonathan, and Shabazz I love you. The results are in, and you all are my biggest supporters. You have my back in ways outsiders could never understand. Y'all shine so brightly in your individual greatness, but you still make time to see my shine. Y'all are the real MVPs.

To my precious grandmothers, Joan Stewart and Delores McCormick, words don't begin to describe my love for you two. I will simply say that I pray I make you proud.

Louise Nichols, you instantly accepted me into your family, and even when circumstances changed, our love remained the same. Thank you for always being there for me.

My newest relatives: Tarsha, Earl, Grandma Ruby, and all my new cousins/aunties/uncles, thank you for welcoming me into the family and treating me as your own.

It is a blessing to have one set of parents who love and encourage you through your life, it is God's abundance when you have two. Earl and Olivia Collins, thank you for accepting me and treating me like a daughter. You are there whenever I call, you are a warrior for my children and a champion for my husband. You have built a strong family and my prayer is that I add to it positively.

Thank you, nieces, and nephews, for loving auntie even when she is being silly and especially when she is in your business and being annoying. Kisses.

My faith has grown deeper due to my spiritual alliances. Pastor Jekia Ledbetter and Victory Ministries of Christ have been here every step of the way. Pastor Ledbetter, you taught me how to pray and introduced me to a God who changed my life. I will always remember the lessons you taught me and will love you unconditionally.

Pastor Lewis Lee and First Lady Zanaida Lee of LS Revival Center, you two have given so much of yourself to my family. Your guidance, friendship, laughter, and even correction are valued. What you do for the community is respected and Bryan and I pray to be as powerful a couple as you are.

# HEAVENLY GLASSES: VISION CHECK

1 FAITH

What is Faith? **Hebrews 11:1** "Now faith is the substance of things hoped for, the evidence of things not seen." **NIV**

Christianity is nothing without faith. Life throws curve balls and many times we are left wondering how we can duck, dodge, or escape the difficulties. Without faith, we would likely accept defeat and give up. That isn't what God wants for us. He truly desires for us to have a great life, enjoy the desires of our hearts, and win every war. **Ecclesiastes 3:12-13** says that enjoying the good of our labor is a gift from God. This means that when we work hard, God desires for us to reap the benefits. He wants us to have joy, but we have to believe that and then go get it.

Greatness is available if we exercise our faith. When you examine that statement alone, you will begin to understand part of the reasons we have tests and trials. When you hear the word exercise, you would think of a workout. If you wanted to exercise your arms, you would lift weights. If you exercise your legs, you may walk on the treadmill or ride a bike. Brain teasers are said to exercise your mind. Whenever you want to exercise something, you tend to use it more, apply pressure and allow that pressure to increase the tolerance or strength of that thing. This is the same thing that happens with our faith.

How do we establish faith?

Faith can be both life-changing and lifesaving, but what if you don't have any? What if you don't believe God to be all that He is? Before anything else, you must establish your faith. You must know who and what God says He is so that you know who and what you can depend on Him to be. People can give you the simple, yet true response, God is everything, but that's not always enough. That answer doesn't help to establish your true belief or faith. You need specifics. God is a provider when you are in need. When someone tells you that, and you experience a moment of need, now you know to call on God, the provider. "God is everything," is the container, now fill it with the specifics. God the provider, keeper, way maker, healer, friend, and comforter goes inside. Because faith is internal, outsiders cannot establish your faith.

FAITH IS BOTH INTERNAL AND ETERNAL

I recommend these three steps to establish your faith. You have to **study**, **speak** and **apply** the word of God.

Study: Read the Bible. The Bible is the basis of our faith. The Bible contains our rules, but it also contains God's promises. **Romans 10:17** says, "So then faith *comes* by hearing, and hearing by the word of God." Strong faith doesn't come just by reading the word of God, it requires you to study.

Think of life as a test and the Bible is the textbook. When you study for a test, you don't just read the textbook. You analyze everything. You never know how the teacher will present the questions and you want to be prepared for all variables. You take your time, and you ensure that you don't miss anything. This is how you approach the Bible. Take your time to truly analyze what was written and allow God to show you how it applies to your life.

Before getting started, pray. Pray that God directs you to the scriptures that you need. Also, pray that He opens your eyes, mind, and heart to the message He intends for you to receive. Two people could read the same scripture and get two different messages. That is because we are all at various places in our lives and walks, but God's word is unchanging. His word encompasses every situation, and it was written so perfectly that we can always apply it to our lives. It's nice to have the man or woman of God teach you about the word, but there is nothing like studying yourself. It's available for you and you don't need to have a fancy degree or extensive vocabulary to understand the messages. God will meet you right where you are and expand your level of understanding because He can do just that. You begin with prayer because you need God to be in control of the entire process.

If you study to only pass the test, the information can be lost after you have achieved your goal. It's more effective to study to learn. Study to retain the knowledge and use it in the future. Meditate on the word of God. Let it reside in you. After you have read the Bible, think about what you have read. God doesn't stop working when the book closes. He can continuously reveal things to you about that scripture, so remain open to receive.

Speak: Speak what you have read. Speak what you have learned. Even if you don't have the strongest faith at the time, you can fake it until you make it. Speak the word of God. Speak it to your friends, strangers, and most importantly speak it to yourself. My grandmother told me that if you tell a lie enough, even you start to believe that it's true. Imagine what can happen when you consistently speak the truth.

The Bible says we are more than conquerors, so tell yourself, I am more than a conqueror. The Bible says that you are the head and not the tail. Take that information, look in the mirror, and say, I am the head and not the tail. **Proverbs 18:21** says, "Death and life *are* in the power of the tongue, And those who love it will eat its fruit." If you speak positive things about yourself, you are speaking the truth. When you speak what the word of God says, you are speaking life. You have done the studying, so you know what was written. Begin speaking, and the believing is sure to follow.

Apply: Apply the word to your daily activities, thoughts, and words. **James 1:22,** "But be doers of the word, and not hearers only, deceiving yourselves."

There are explicit instructions in the Bible about how we should live and carry ourselves. We are also told to be loving, kind, honest, and giving. We are told who we are in Christ. We are overcomers, we are of a royal bloodline, and we are chosen. We are told to study the word, spread the gospels, and worship and praise God. The Bible is filled with instructions and love. If you follow the instructions, receive the love, and live a God-approved life, you will begin to see God's promises being fulfilled in your life. When you see God do exactly what He said he would do, faith is established.

How do we exercise our faith?

You must be placed in positions that will push you to operate in faith more. God can be viewed as the personal trainer. He will allow trials to come so that pressure may be applied. We exercise our faith by remaining positive through every situation. Instead of crying in pain, we cry out in praise. We thank God for the breakthrough that we haven't received. We thank God for being debt-free when the turn-off notices arrive. This is allowing our faith to replace fear.

Why are the struggles getting more extreme and continuously coming, after you have overcome them by faith?

If we go back to the arms example, once your arm has increased in strength, you apply heavier weights. The only way to go to the next level is if the task gets harder. When you use your faith to overcome, your faith grows. What's thrown at you next may be more challenging than the last, but that's because you have to increase the pressure to increase your faith.

James 1:3, "knowing that the testing of your faith produces patience. **4** But let patience have *its* perfect work, that you may be perfect and complete, lacking nothing."

Our faith is going to be tested in multiple ways, but those tests serve a purpose. **1 Peter 1:7,** "that the genuineness of your faith, *being* much more precious than gold that perishes, though it is tested by fire, may be found to praise, honor, and glory at the revelation of Jesus Christ..." Gold is a precious metal and for gold to be purified (remove contaminants,) it has to go through the fire. **1 Peter,** says that our faith is MORE precious than gold. So, if gold, which is not as precious as our faith, must endure the fire, what more do you expect our faith to endure. Stay the course, do not give up, and watch your faith grow.

Faith at Work

There is an abundance of examples of faith working in the Bible and here are a few.

Matthew 9:20-22 discusses a woman who had been bleeding for 12 years. She believed that if she could get close enough to touch Jesus, she could be healed. When she grabbed His garment, Jesus turned around and addressed her. He said, "Be of good cheer, daughter; your faith has made you well. And the woman was made well from that hour." He didn't say, I have made you well. He didn't say, a miracle has made you well. We know that Jesus is the one who had the power, but He specified that by her faith she was made well.

This isn't the only instance in the Bible where faith has healed. **Matthew 9:27-30** talks about the two blind men who followed Jesus for healing. They cried out for Jesus to have mercy on them, and He asked them if they believed that He could heal them. They replied yes and Jesus said, "According to your faith let it be so." Their eyes were opened because of their faith.

If God said that you would be successful, healed, happy, married, free or overcome according to your faith, would it happen? Do you trust your faith? If not, go back to the steps listed to establish your faith, and exercise your faith so that then you can experience total victory BECAUSE of your faith.

Prayer

God, I pray that you will increase my faith. Instill in me faith so real and so strong that it has no choice but to grow as my days go on. Protect my mind from doubt and disbelief. Let no thought that is unlike you enter and remove every uncertainty. Prepare me for the battles ahead, trusting and believing that you will guide my steps. God, your word says that all we need is faith the size of a mustard seed, and today I am pleading with you to grow my faith. Pour down your blessings so that I may see the manifestation of faith. So that I may have a reference point of my faith working. God, I pray you to increase my faith and increase my trust in You. In the name of Jesus, I pray these things. Amen.

CHAPTER 1 RECAP

Takeaway: Your faith grows through tests and trials. It is challenging and may be painful, however, God will reward you for remaining faithful in the midst of it all.

Scriptures:

Hebrews 11:1 Now faith is the substance of things hoped for, the evidence of things not seen.

Ecclesiastes 3:12-13 know that nothing *is* better for them than to rejoice, and to do good in their lives, ¹³ and also that every man should eat and drink and enjoy the good of all his labor—it *is* the gift of God.

Romans 10:17 So then faith *comes* by hearing and hearing by the word of God.

Proverbs 18:21 Death and life *are* in the power of the tongue, And those who love it will eat its fruit.

James 1:22 But be doers of the word, and not hearers only, deceiving yourselves.

James 1:3-4 knowing that the testing of your faith

produces patience. ⁴ But let patience have *its* perfect work, that you may be perfect and complete, lacking nothing.

1 Peter 1:7 that the genuineness of your faith, *being* much more precious than gold that perishes, though it is tested by fire, may be found to praise, honor, and glory at the revelation of Jesus Christ

Matthew 9:20-22 And suddenly, a woman who had a flow of blood for twelve years came from behind and touched the hem of His garment. ²¹ For she said to herself, "If only I may touch His garment, I shall be made well." ²² But Jesus turned around, and when He saw her He said, "Be of good cheer, daughter; your faith has made you well." And the woman was made well from that hour.

Matthew 9:27-30 When Jesus departed from there, two blind men followed Him, crying out and saying, "Son of David, have mercy on us!"

²⁸ And when He had come into the house, the blind men came to Him. And Jesus said to

them, "Do you believe that I can do this?"

They said to Him, "Yes, Lord."

29 Then He touched their eyes, saying, "According to your faith let it be to you." **30** And their eyes were opened. And Jesus sternly warned them, saying, "See *that* no one knows *it*."

Vision Check: Do you believe God for whatever you need? Do you believe that He will supply you with the desires of your heart? Do you doubt God? Frequently do a faith check on yourself and look back at your reference points when your faith begins to waver.

2 GPS

Scripture: Psalms 5:8 Lead me, Lord, in your righteousness because of my enemies- make your way straight before me. **NIV**

Message: Consult with God before making moves in life and allow Him to direct your path.

My husband is better than me with directions. If you show him one time, and he's paying attention, he usually retains the directions for the future. Me on the other hand, I'm horrible. I have to use my GPS to get just about everywhere.

There are places, like my children's schools, where I know exactly how to get there. For years, I've jumped in my car, usually running a little late, and headed the way I know. I was a bit discombobulated a few months ago. I was experiencing different stressors and when I got in the car to pick them up from school, something made me put the address in my GPS. To my surprise, it directed me to a different route than I would usually travel. I said to myself, "I know how to get there." Then I proceeded to go the way that I knew. I followed the instructions I had grown comfortable with. Can you guess what happened? There was traffic. As I sat there, now running late for pickup, it hit me! If I had listened to the GPS, I would have been on time.

Although being sent on an unusual path, it was the fastest route. It was the fastest because the original route had an accident. There was an avoidable delay that I was being protected from. This situation made me think about God and how He's willing and trying to guide us, but we won't turn to him. We are so determined to do what we know is right, but the funny thing is we don't know anything. We think we know everything but there are so many unexpected variables that we don't consider.

God is the one who knows what's going to happen before it happens. He knows the way for us to go to avoid hurt and he also knows what choice we will make and how to guide us through. The GPS also makes you aware of tolls, highways, and other inconveniences. God is the ultimate GPS.

Now, regardless of where I'm going, I turn to my GPS. I check in to ensure that there are no delays that I'm unable to see from my position. I want to know if there will be any inconveniences along the route I chose and I want to know the fastest route.

If you consult God before everything, big or minor, you can't go wrong. Let Him guide you. Let Him tell you the safest and fastest route with the least inconveniences. Allow God to do one of the things He does best, guide your steps. Saying that you consult God before every decision is easy, but this requires two steps. The first is to consult him, the second is to do what He says. Go where He leads and say what he commands you to say. It may be uncomfortable for you, but when you stray from the GPS, you usually encounter a delay to your destiny.

When I see or think of GPS, I now think of it as God's Positioning System. Declare today that you will follow the GPS and trust and believe that God will carry you through.

Prayer

God, I pray that I am open and available to go where you lead me. Give me the courage to follow you even when the road looks scary or when I'm not sure of the destination. Help me to recognize when you are protecting me. I want to trust in you enough to blindly follow you. Help me, dear God, to grow and become that person. In Jesus' name, Amen.

EBONY COLLINS

3 PRIDE

Scripture: Proverbs 16:18 Pride goes before destruction, a haughty spirit before a fall. **NIV**

Message: Being full of pride is being void of God's blessings.

Natural Eyes: Being independent is something that we take immense pride in. As a black woman, I can only speak for myself, but I was taught to never depend on others. If you depend on others, they can disappoint you or inconvenience you and that was never a risk worth taking. The inconvenience comes when you end up having to do it yourself because the task wasn't completed properly. To protect ourselves from all the possible negativity, we do everything ourselves. Sometimes we don't ask for help because we don't want others to know that we are in need. We don't want people to see our inadequacies and weaknesses. We are just too proud.

Heavenly Glasses: Years ago, a young pastor taught a bible study lesson on pride, and he introduced me to a new way of thinking. He taught about the pride that we are all used to hearing about. Thinking so highly of yourself and disregarding the role that God plays in it all. He taught on how it's important to understand that we are nothing without God and His grace and mercy. As he spoke, I sat there shaking my head in agreement. I was thinking, "Oh, I thank and give God credit for everything. That's the one sin I know I'm free of. I'm confident in this pride thing. I'm as humble as can be. God has worked on me with this pride thing, I'm good." Seriously, those were my thoughts.

Then he said he was going to give us another example of what pride looks like. I put my pen down because I knew what pride was. This lesson wasn't for me tonight. I'm sure we've all had those moments where we sat in church and knew that the preacher wasn't walking down our street and then BAM, our toes were stepped on. The next thing he said danced all over my bare feet. He said that pride is refusing to ask for help. My mouth dropped open. This is one of my biggest downfalls. I never viewed this as a downfall but a skill, a quality. Being self-sufficient and independent was one of my best qualities. At times, it still is. I was taught that if I wanted something done correctly, I would be better off doing it myself. My experience had shown me that it was better to struggle to do it alone than to ask for assistance from people who could someday throw it back in my face. I hated the idea of people talking about the things they had done for me and then acting as if I owed them something. Due to all the reasons listed above, I did most things on my own.

It was explained that this thought process was full of pride because we weren't valuing God's people as high as we valued ourselves. Not trusting that you can depend on someone or that they will complete the task is saying that you're the only one capable. What does that say about all who He created? In a sense, it is saying that I am better than you, so I won't ever ask for help.

When we don't ask for help because we don't want people to see us in need or vulnerable, that's also pride. We are all created equally, and we all need one another. If we resist help not only, are we making things harder for ourselves, but we are telling God that we don't trust that He knew what He was doing in creation. We tell him that we are greater than what He put in place for us and that we know better on our own.

Our heavenly glasses will allow us to break away from the bondage of pride and to recognize when we need what someone else has. If you are stuck in a place and need help breaking free, reach out to God's people. Let someone know that you need help or that you are suffering so that healing will take place.

Proverbs 16:18 says Pride goes before destruction, a haughty spirit before a fall. This scripture is warning us that destruction comes after pride. Heed the warning and know the signs of pride. If I had died before hearing that teaching, years ago, I would have surely seen destruction because I was living a prideful life and didn't know. I'm here to tell you to examine what pride is and remove it from your life. Being unable to request and accept help is being unable to receive God's blessings. Make yourself available for your blessing.

Prayer

God, I thank you for being you. I thank you for your power, your grace, and your mercy. I thank you for your wisdom and strength. I pray that you open my mind and heart to help. Remove the spirit of control from my mind. Remove the negative thoughts of people not being willing or able to help me from my mind. Humble me, Lord. Take the pride away that's hiding within. The pride that I don't think I have. Please forgive me for all the prideful moments or thoughts that I have had. Forgive me for my lack of knowledge and understanding. Forgive me for my lack of trust in you and what you have created. I love you and all those who represent you. Help me grow my trust in you which will help me grow my trust in people. Make the walls of my defenses crumble but also surround me with trustworthy people. People who will willingly help when called on. I thank you in advance, God. In Jesus' name, Amen.

Chapter 3 Recap

Takeaway: It's ok to ask for and accept help from others.

Scripture:

Proverbs 16:18 Pride goes before destruction, a haughty spirit before a fall.

Hebrews 13:6 "Don't forget to do good and to share what you have because God is pleased with these kinds of sacrifices."

Romans 12:13 "Contribute to the needs of God's people, and welcome strangers into your home."

Vision Check: If you find yourself hesitating to ask for help when you are in need, check yourself. Get to the root of the hesitation and remind yourself that we all need one another. We all depend on each other to be successful in life. Most importantly, God placed us all here to lean on one another.

EBONY COLLINS

4 LET GO

Scripture: Luke 9:62 Jesus replied, "No one who puts a hand to the plow and looks back is fit for service in the kingdom of God." **NIV**

Message: When God calls you out of things, don't look back. Walk towards where God called you, without the distractions of where He pulled you from.

Natural Eyes: When God calls us away from a person, place, or thing, we may encounter internal resistance. We get comfortable where we are regardless of the circumstances. I've heard people say that they would rather stay in the craziness that they are familiar with, instead of moving on to a potential crazy. This is especially spoken in unhealthy relationships. People use familiarity to justify staying where they don't belong. They are accustomed to the negativity and have begun to normalize it in their minds. It's easy to stay where you are because you have produced a million ways to cope, and you become content. The problem comes when God tells you to move. This message can come through a dream, a whispered word, a messenger being used, or writing on a wall. Regardless of how it is delivered, people still have problems moving and not looking back.

Heavenly Glasses: Recognize that when God calls you to leave something or someone behind, it is for your good. He is typically protecting you from something or elevating you to something greater. By looking back, you are indicating that you can't let go. You are showing that you value that of the past more than what God has in store for your future.

God sent two angels to destroy Sodom and Gomorrah because their sin was so great. When they arrived, Lot found favor with the angels. He took them in and protected them. This gave pause to their mission and Lot was allowed to take his family and flee from his home. (This is discussed more in chapter **12 Entertaining Angels**.) Lot had a wife, future sons-in-law, and two daughters. When Lot told the sons in law, that they must flee, they didn't believe him. Because they doubted him, they were left behind to be destroyed with the city. His daughters and wife believed him and allowed the angels to lead them away.

How many times have we remained stagnated when God gave a command because others refused to obey? Imagine if Lot's daughters had stayed behind because of love for their men. How many places have you stayed because of love when God told you to move?

They were all told to not look back and to continue or they too would be swept away. Lot's wife looked back and was turned into a pillar of salt. Maybe she needed to see what was happening for herself. It's possible that she wanted to see if anyone else was coming. It's possible she thought she left something behind. It doesn't matter why she looked back, what matters is that she did not stay focused on where she was being called to go. She lost sight of the mission ahead. Instead, she looked back to the past.

If God wanted you to be concerned with the places of the past, He would have left you there. We leave relationships and then stalk their social media accounts for updates. If God wanted you with them, you would have been left in the relationship. Move on and don't look back! How can you give your present life or your future 100% if you are still giving 25% to yesterday?

> **If God wanted you to be concerned with the places of the past, He would have left you there.**

How do you forget about the past? You don't. It happened and it is ingrained in our memories. There were both good and bad days and each experience helped to shape our beings. The true charge is to not dwell on the past. When you invest your time and energy into thinking about yesterday, today suffers and tomorrow may never come. Allow the people that God removed from your life to exist without you. Don't be concerned with what they are doing or how they are living. When you are called away from a job, don't sit around imagining how you would have progressed in the company had you stayed. Let it go! Place your energy in the NOW! Trust that God has a plan for you in your current place.

What do you do when the people you love refuse to go along with God's command? Leave them. The sons-in-law would not listen to Lot, so he left them. His wife turned back, so he continued without her. You cannot allow yourself to get caught up in who didn't join you on the journey, just be grateful that you were wise enough to push forward.

This may seem easier said than done, but no one said that living a life for God was supposed to be easy. Leaving people behind is supposed to affect us because we are human. It just isn't supposed to stop us!

Handling Death

Sometimes we lose loved ones because they have gone on to be with the Lord(prayerfully). In these situations, we grieve the loss as we should. I would never tell you to just, let it go, however you still must live. In remembering Lot's wife, the Bible states that she looked back and turned into a pillar of salt, but he and his daughters continued. You never really hear her mentioned again. Lot and his daughters continued to live, even though they experienced a great loss. I am sure there was sadness, grief, and sorrow felt, but it wasn't discussed. They had to continue living. Had the chapter dwelled on their emotions, we would have missed everything that followed.

The Bible tells us in **Ecclesiastes 3,** that there is a time to be born and a time to die. Once a person's time has expired on earth, God calls them back. He is lending our loved ones to us.

When you are amid the hurt, it seems like all words and clichés. Imagine if you could adjust your thinking to the point that you believe the truth. It would still hurt to lose people; however, we would trust fully that it was in God's divine plan.

Luke 9:59-60, Jesus told a man to follow Him, and the man wanted to first bury his father. Jesus told him to let the dead worry about the dead but commanded the man to go and proclaim the kingdom of God. This is a reminder that you can't allow death to stop your work for God.

You can't allow your grief to stifle your progress. Your loved one died, you did not. This is a hard truth to swallow. We are human and we feel. There is no requirement to turn those feelings off, however, we must control what we do with them. Allow those feelings to propel you closer to God. Allow those emotions to push you into your destiny.

Luke 9:61-62, talks about a man Jesus told to follow Him and the man wanted to go back and say goodbye to his family. Jesus told him that anyone who turns back is not fit for service.

Be ready when Jesus calls you. Sometimes we will leave with no explanation, no goodbye, and no farewell hugs, but we must go. Jesus calls us and we answer. There is no time to look back. Allow yourself to feel but refuse to get stuck.

Prayer

God, I pray that you open me up to understand why people that I love couldn't join me in the next chapter of my life. I pray that you heal the hurt that comes from missing them and not understanding. I pray that you bless them abundantly in all that they do. Open my eyes and heart to truly realize that they were here with me for a season and a reason and now, as I walk into a new season, they could not come along. God, I thank you for the time that I shared with them. I thank you for all that they contributed to me and my life. I pray that we have peace, knowing that you still sit on the throne. Knowing that everything you do is strategic and for our benefit. I thank you for all things. In Jesus' name, Amen.

Grief Prayer

God, I pray that you heal my heart from the hurt of loss. I know that you only loan people to us for a short while, but oh how I love them. Please send the Holy Spirit to comfort me, to console me, and give me the warmth that I am missing. God be my comfort during this time. Be my peace. In Jesus' name, Amen.

Chapter 4 Recap

Takeaway: Although difficult, you must let the past live in the past, or else you can never move to your future.

Scriptures:

Genesis 19 discusses what Lot had to leave behind in detail.

Luke 9:62 Jesus replied, "No one who puts a hand to the plow and looks back is fit for service in the kingdom of God."

Vision Check: Has God told you to move, and others questioned your actions? Don't be deterred from doing the will of God or you will be stuck in what you have always known. You must move differently to get different results. People that you care about may not understand your why for certain things, but you must stay strong, and do exactly what God told you, even if you can't explain it to others.

5 JUDAS

Scripture: Matthew 26:53 Do you think I cannot call on my Father, and he will at once put at my disposal more than twelve legions of angels? **54** But how then would the Scriptures be fulfilled that say it must happen in this way?" **NIV**

Message: Your purpose cannot be achieved without your Judas.

Natural Eyes: In the natural, once you feel that you have given your trust to someone and they betray you, they immediately become the enemy. We search for the reason behind their betrayal, trying to figure out if we contributed somehow. This can send you into a rage, confusion, and even depression.

Heavenly Glasses: Change your perception of the "betrayer," to allow your life to flow with less animosity and stress. Instead of trying to figure out why the person did what they did, accept that it was their purpose, to push you into yours. Remember Judas. Because Jesus was crucified, we are forgiven and set free of our sins. Because Judas betrayed Jesus, Jesus was crucified. This is the Judas effect, and it can be applied to all our lives. This is not to say that all the people in your life that bring hurt, or deception are assigned to do it, but all of it was allowed. As learned with Job, nothing can happen to us unless God allows it. He is the supreme authority of all things.

When we enter relationships with people, we hope they treat us with the love and respect that we give them, but that's not always the reality. When these people turn on you, take it as a lesson and move on. Live your life because Judas didn't end Jesus' story. He pushed Him to the next level and fulfilled the prophesy which caused Jesus to walk out His purpose.

Jesus knew that Judas would be the one to betray Him, but we don't always recognize our Judas before the attack.

When you realize that someone has betrayed you, what should you do?

If we follow Jesus' lead in **Matthew 26:24**, we realize that it is not necessary to retaliate. That person will get what is coming to them and you don't have to be the one to deliver the punishment. That is one of the best parts of living a life for Christ. You don't have to hand out punishments, but you can rest assured that they will be handled.

Is Judas bad?

The answer to this is a matter of opinion. When I look at Judas, I see someone who was destined to betray. I see someone who pushed Jesus to where God already assigned Him to go. Someone else may only view Judas as the person who had the son of God killed. I challenge you to be encouraged and know that because it was allowed, it will be used to build you up.

How do you recognize your Judas?

Unlike Jesus, many times we don't know our Judas upon sight. We look back on a situation and our interactions with a person and recognize what they did. Then we need to evaluate what occurred because of their betrayal. Did you grow? Did you learn? That person can be viewed as your Judas, which means they were necessary for your life.

Prayer

God, I pray that you allow me to see people for who they truly are and what their purpose is in my life. I pray that you give me the strength to persevere through the hurt of betrayal and the wisdom to transform my disappointment in others into energy and courage for climbing to the next level in you. Heal the hurt that they caused. Restore my peace Lord and restore my joy. Open my eyes to see situations for what they are and open my heart to accept your will and way. Knowing that you make no mistakes, and all things are allowed through you, I thank you in advance. I pray these things in Jesus' name, Amen.

Chapter 5 Recap

Takeaway: Betrayal can push you to your blessing.

Scripture:

Matthew 26:21 And while they were eating, he said, "Truly I tell you, one of you will betray me."

Matthew 26:24 The Son of Man will go just as it is written about him. But woe to that man who betrays the Son of Man! It would be better for him if he had not been born."

Matthew 26:53 Do you think I cannot call on my Father, and he will at once put at my disposal more than twelve legions of angels? **54** But how then would the Scriptures be fulfilled that say it must happen in this way?"

Vision Check: Has anyone ever betrayed you? Has someone done something to destroy you? How did that make you feel and what did it make you do? Typically, it makes you try harder and do better. We don't want people to know that they are affecting us, so we get stronger when they try to break us down. Your Judas is pushing you.

6 UNEXPECTED HARDSHIPS

Scripture: Job 1:8 Then the Lord said to Satan, "Have you considered my servant Job? There is no one on earth like him; he is blameless and upright, a man who fears God and shuns evil." **NIV**

Message: You were chosen for this.

Natural Eyes: When you examine all that you experience in the natural, it's easy to get confused and even discouraged. You look back and realize that you have been faithful to God and living according to His word, yet you are struggling. You are honest and committed, you spread the gospel and you help others, yet you experience lack. You feed the hungry, clothe the poor, attend church every Sunday and join different ministries, yet you are hurting. You visit the prayer line weekly and go to your prayer closet, crying out to God but you see no resolution for your problem. When you feel like you are doing everything right, but are still experiencing the difficulties of life, you can easily feel God has forsaken you. It's natural to believe that God is cruel and unloving. I wouldn't even be surprised if you questioned His existence.

Heavenly Glasses: The problem with allowing your natural feelings, questions, and concerns to pollute your mind is that we are not fighting a natural battle. I challenge you to remove your, why me shades, and to equip yourself with your, it's a privilege and an honor glasses. Your heavenly glasses will allow you to see that Satan is always on the prowl looking for who he can pull away from God. He doesn't need to fight for the people who are serving him, and he doesn't want the ones who are serving anyone other than God. He wants to steal the ones who are serving the true and living God. They say to be the best, you must beat the best, and who is better than God?

If you are being tested, there is something special bubbling inside of you that the enemy wants to crush. Your purpose, gifts, and destiny are what made you eligible for your struggle. God's grace, mercy, and His favor are what ensure your total victory. (This is discussed more in **Chapter 13 The Book of Job**.)

The first thing that happens is the enemy travels the earth looking for who he may convert. The Bible says in **John 10:10** that he comes to *steal*, *kill,* and *destroy*. He wants to steal God's people, kill their faith, and destroy their purpose.

Steal – (Genesis 1:27) The enemy wants to steal us because we are created in God's image. Satan wants to be above God so he naturally wants who belongs to God. **

Kill – (Matthew 17:20) The enemy wants to kill your faith. The Bible says that faith the size of a mustard seed can move mountains. Faith will make you stay loyal to God. If your faith is broken your loyalty is broken.**

Destroy – (Jeremiah 1:5) You had a purpose before you were born. God has a great purpose for you and if the enemy can separate you from your purpose he has won.**

Next, God chooses whom He will allow to face the trials. Satan thinks he is choosing, but God selects you. He selects you because he knows that your faith is sufficient, and your purpose is perfect.

He knows that you can handle what you are about to face.

Then, you go through. God allows the struggles and stress. He permits the drama and pain. You exercise or activate your faith and then you win.

Your hardships were designed for you to overcome. These tests were set up to provide you with a reference point. The next time that you experience a rough patch, commit it to memory. Then, when issues come, you can look back and remember, God can pull you through. Remember that you were victorious before and you will be victorious again. Not only *can* God pull you through, but He will also pull you through.

PRAYER

God, I'm going through and it hurts. I know that your word said that you would never leave me nor forsake me, but I'm feeling alone. I know your word said that you would be my provider but I'm experiencing a lack. You said to come to you even in my challenging times, but I'm tired. I read you would give me strength, but I'm weakened. God, I need you now! I need you on this day, at this moment. The enemy is running rampant in my life. I'm sinking and I know that you are my life source, but it's so hard to reach out. Reach to me God, grab me, God. Help me! I need to see a supernatural turnaround of events. I need change. I need improvement. I thank you today for what I know only you can do in my life. In Jesus' name, Amen.

EBONY COLLINS

Chapter 6 Recap

Takeaway: You were chosen for this test BECAUSE you are strong enough to pass.

Scripture:

Matthew 17:20 He replied, "Because you have so little faith. Truly I tell you, if you have faith as small as a mustard seed, you can say to this mountain, 'Move from here to there,' and it will move. Nothing will be impossible for you."

Genesis 1:27 So God created mankind in his image, in the image of God he created them; male and female he created them.

Jeremiah 1:5 Before I formed you in the womb I knew you, before you were born I set you apart; I appointed you as a prophet to the nations.

Job 1:8 Then the Lord said to Satan, "Have you considered my servant Job? There is no one on earth like him; he is blameless and upright, a man who fears God and shuns evil.

Vision Check: Have you ever gone through a rough time in the past? Did you survive? I can guarantee that the answer to both of those questions is yes. Keep in mind that if God fixed it before, He will fix it again. He loves you enough that He wants you to win, so you will.

7 FORGIVENESS

Scripture: **Micah 7:18-19: 18** Who is a god like you, who pardons sin and forgives the transgression of the remnant of his inheritance? You do not stay angry forever but delight to show mercy. **19** you will again have compassion on us; you will tread our sins underfoot and hurl all our iniquities into the depths of the sea. **NIV**

Message: Forgiveness is a me thing.

Natural Eyes: When someone hurts or offends us, we are left feeling disappointed or angry. We then allow that anger to rise within us. Whether or not an apology is issued, before granting forgiveness, we tend to analyze if they are worthy of forgiveness. Will they hurt me again? Is the apology genuine?

Will I look foolish to others if I forgive them? If they embarrassed me publicly, shouldn't they apologize publicly? Don't forget the famous, forgive but never forget phrase. We place all types of stipulations and rules on forgiveness because we are looking at it all wrong.

Heavenly Glasses: We get stuck evaluating how worthy a person is of forgiveness and forget who forgiveness is about. When someone does something to hurt you, they must live with that. If they lie on you, spread rumors, cheat, or steal from you, that is their burden to bear. They are fully aware of what they have done and honestly, they don't need your forgiveness. They did what they did, if they have a conscience, it's tormenting them. If they don't, God will still handle them. They continue living but you remain bound by the hurt.

Forgiveness frees you from bearing the burden of someone else's wrongdoing. When you can truly forgive someone, you move on from the situation and experience peace. When you hold on, you are holding onto all the negative emotions associated with what they did. Releasing the negative makes room for the love that God has waiting for you.

The Bible talks about forgiveness in multiple scriptures. **Matthew 18:21-35** begins with Jesus telling Peter to forgive his brother 77 times. This doesn't mean that we need to keep count of how many times someone does wrong and once we reach 77, forgiveness ends. This is just an indication that we need to forgive repeatedly. There isn't a magic number for forgiveness. If there were then we would have lost our access to the kingdom long ago. Just forgive. Easier said than done? Of course, it is, but forgiveness should get easier when you change your perception. Living a life pleasing to God gets easier when you view life the way God does.

    Staying with the same scripture, examine the servant. The servant owed a debt to the king and begged for more time to pay, instead of punishment. The king felt pity for him and canceled his debt. He forgave him. The servant went out and ran into a fellow servant who owed him, and that servant had the same request. He requested more time instead of punishment. Well, the servant who was forgiven by the king was not as kind when he was in the position of power. He had the man thrown into prison. Right there, the forgiven servant had a choice. Would he give what he had been given, forgiveness and grace, or would he be hateful? You have a choice too. Our father, God, has forgiven us, will you forgive others?

    There was a choice to be made and the one that he made changed his course. When the king heard about what had occurred, he called the servant he had already forgiven back to him. He told him that because he did not forgive his fellow servant after he had been forgiven, he would now be thrown in prison and tortured. Because he could not forgive, he would suffer punishment.

Imagine if your forgiveness from God was dependent on your ability to forgive your fellow man. Not just say you forgive, but to truly forgive people in your heart. Holding onto hurt will cause you to miss blessings and forfeit your joy and peace. Peace cannot reside where bitterness lives.

If we were to forgive how God forgives, there would be no record of wrongs. The Bible says in **Micah 7:19**, that our sins are thrown into the depths of the sea. He is a compassionate God, a loving God, and a forgiving God. Your heavenly glasses will remind you that God created the world and everything that it consists of. He created the birds and the trees. He created the land and the sky. He created you and me. He is the God of ALL creation. He is perfect in all His ways. Yet we still sin against Him. In all His perfection, we sin, and we disobey Him. Then what does God do? He forgives us and throws our iniquities into the depths of the sea. We dare to walk around like we are more important than Him and so special that we cannot forgive someone who has wronged us.

Your unhappiness can be coming from your inability to let go of what others did to you. Forgiving doesn't make you weak, it means you are strong enough to choose yourself. You are strong enough to put both, your mental and spiritual health first.

FORGIVING SELF

We all make choices and because of those choices, we face consequences. There can be positive consequences or negative consequences depending on the situation. When we have negative consequences, we face the what-ifs? What if I had done this differently? What if I had made a different decision? What if I had never said that? What if I didn't quit the job? What if I didn't tell that lie? What if I had answered the phone? Get all of that out of your head. Throw the what if's, away because you cannot go back and redo the past. You will never know what could have been different, so operate on what you do know. You know that you made a decision. The decision produced disappointing results, and now you must learn how to move forward appropriately.

Forgiving ourselves can prove to be more challenging than forgiving others. We hold ourselves to a higher standard because we know our potential. The truth is, if you can't forgive yourself, how can you genuinely love yourself? Forgiving yourself doesn't mean that you didn't do anything wrong or don't deserve any consequences. Forgiving yourself means that you acknowledge what you did was wrong, and you have gone to God and repented. It means that you will make a conscious effort to do better, be better, and live better.

When you hold grudges against yourself, you are constantly looking for, and accepting what you deem to be punishment. You allow people to mistreat you because you feel you deserve it. The devil is a liar. You deserve all the greatness that God has to offer. You deserve loyalty, dedication, and love. You deserve peace, joy, and most of all, you deserve all the forgiveness that it is commanded of you to give others. Stop accepting whatever people are willing to give you. Stop beating yourself up over what you did or should have done. Release that into the sea of forgetfulness and move forward in the greatness that is mercy.

Prayer

Oh, most gracious, merciful God, I thank you. I praise your holy name, giving you all the honor that is owed to you. I come to you with a humble heart. I come to you with full repentance. I pray that the forgiveness that was promised to me, be delivered. I pray that you soften my heart so that I may truly and fully forgive those who have wronged me. Touch those people so that they may realize the error in their ways, and they may live a more Christ-like life. Touch them to be free from the bondage of their transgressions. Touch them in a way that they know it was you. Now, God, I pray that you help me to forgive myself. I messed up, but I need a peace that can't be shaken to dwell within me, despite me. God, I trust you for these things that I have asked. In Jesus' name, Amen.

EBONY COLLINS

Chapter 7 Recap

Takeaway: You gain more than you lose when you forgive.

Scriptures:

MICAH 7:18-19 who is a god like you, who pardons sin and forgives the transgression of the remnant of his inheritance? You do not stay angry forever but delight to show mercy. **19** you will again have compassion on us; you will tread our sins underfoot and hurl all our iniquities into the depths of the sea.

Matthew 18:21-22 **21** Then Peter came to Jesus and asked, "Lord, how many times shall I forgive my brother or sister who sins against me? Up to seven times?" **22** Jesus answered, "I tell you, not seven times, but seventy-seven times.

Matthew 18:32-35 **32** "Then the master called the servant in. 'You wicked servant,' he said, 'I canceled all that debt of yours because you begged me to. **33** Shouldn't you have had mercy on your fellow servant just as I had on you?' **34** In anger his master handed him over to the jailers to be tortured until he should pay back all he owed.

[35] "This is how my heavenly Father will treat each of you unless you forgive your brother or sister from your heart."

Vision Check:

1. When you see the person who did something to hurt you, do you get angry?

2. When you think about the person or the situation, do you have negative thoughts?

3. When you find out that positive things have happened for that person, do you feel that they don't deserve it?

4. Do you believe that bad things are happening in your life as a result of something you did in the past?

5. Have you EVER done anything and been granted forgiveness?

If you answer yes to questions 1-4, RELEASE. Release what was done to you and release what you have done to others. Release it, grant forgiveness, and live in the fullness that is God's grace and mercy.

8 DREAM KILLERS

Scripture: **Genesis 37:19** "Here comes that dreamer!" they said to each other. **20** "Come now, let's kill him and throw him into one of these cisterns and say that a ferocious animal devoured him. Then we'll see what comes of his dreams." **NIV**

Message: If God whispered it to you in a dream, don't be so eager to shout it while awake.

Natural Eyes: God revealed something to you in a dream and it has not happened. All you can see are the obstacles preventing you from achieving what you know is supposed to be yours. Every time you get closer to what you know to be your destiny, you are derailed. It seems like the people closest to you are working against you, and the ones who love you have set out to destroy you. Now, you are in a place wondering if you really heard from God. You begin to question if you even want what was promised.

Heavenly Glasses: In **Genesis 37:5**, Joseph has a dream that indicated his brothers, mother, and father would all bow down to him. The fact that he has the dream isn't where the problem occurs. The true problem is what he does next. It says, he told his brothers and they hated him.

It's important to understand that everyone doesn't need to know what was told to you in private. Treat God the way you want to be treated. If you promise one child something, you may not tell the others, because you know that they can't handle knowing that they won't receive the same as their sibling. We are God's children. Sometimes our siblings cannot understand why He chose us to receive certain blessings.

If you continue reading, not only did Joseph's brothers take issue with what Joseph dreamed, but his father rebuked him. Joseph should have kept quiet.

Because of their hatred towards Joseph, their fear of his dreams, and their envy of his destiny, his brothers set him up for what was supposed to be his downfall. *people are plotting on your failure*
Beginning at **Genesis 37:12**, Joseph's brothers

went out to graze their father's flock. Joseph was sent to find them. When they saw Joseph coming, they began to plot on him.

Can you imagine how many people hear your dreams and begin plotting against you? It's not a result of anything that you have done or said, it's jealousy. They associate your success with their inability to achieve. They have convinced themselves that your destiny blocks theirs. What needs to be realized is that what God has for them is for them. More importantly, no matter what they do, they can never have what God has designed for someone else. When you try to destroy someone else's destiny, you block yours.

One of Joseph's brothers spoke up and convinced the brothers not to kill him. Instead, his brothers ended up selling him to the Ishmaelites. They sold him for twenty shekels of silver. *Someone is underestimating your value* I can tell you now, they didn't fully understand Joseph's worth.

They thought they killed his dreams and destroyed his purpose, but they had no idea that as long as the man lives, God's will shall be done. You can't kill purpose without killing the man. **As long as you live, God will take every situation and use it to push you into your destiny. ***

Although God will use everything for your good, why do we have to make things so difficult? Stop sharing everything that God tells you. Trust Him, be excited about your destiny, but be private about your conversations. Everyone doesn't mean you good. Sometimes, it's the people closest to you, people you've met in passing, or even co-workers who want to stop you. Sometimes, we don't know who is preying on us, instead of praying for us. For this reason, you must guard the promises of God. Guard your destiny and guard your purpose.

I always find it interesting to see what people hold near to them. You can't ask a person how much money they have in their bank account because they have a fear of you robbing them, which would jeopardize their future. If not, they fear you know too much about their finances, trying to spend their money, or becoming envious if they are wealthier than you. Why do we not think that people can become this way about their God-promised future? When your faith is strong, and your belief in God is real, you treat Him and all things concerning Him as a priority.

Joseph was sold, but this isn't where his story ends. He was then given over to Potiphar, one of Pharaoh's officials and captain of the Guard. The story of Joseph will allow you to see how God can and will use every situation for your good when you are chosen. **(Continue to Chapter 9: Delay Not Denial for the conclusion).**

PRAYER

God, I'm so excited about your promises to me. I receive every word you have spoken in my ear. If it is for me to keep to myself, I pray you give me the patience to be still and silent. I pray that you continue to reveal things to me, and I will keep those things in confidence. I thank you for trusting me enough with your secrets and trusting me enough with your plans for my life. Now, God, I pray that those who seek to destroy me be stopped in their tracks. I pray that you block every attack of the enemy, every obstacle, every evil that tries to rise. Block it before it can even reach me, Lord. Be my rod and my staff, be my shield, be my comfort. In Jesus' name, Amen.

CHAPTER 8 RECAP

Takeaway: Don't share your dreams with everyone.

Scriptures:

Genesis 37:5-11 ⁵ Joseph had a dream, and when he told it to his brothers, they hated him all the more. ⁶ He said to them, "Listen to this dream I had: ⁷ We were binding sheaves of grain out in the field when suddenly my sheaf rose and stood upright, while your sheaves gathered around mine and bowed down to it."

⁸ His brothers said to him, "Do you intend to reign over us? Will you actually rule us?" And they hated him all the more because of his dream and what he had said.

⁹ Then he had another dream, and he told it to his brothers. "Listen," he said, "I had another dream, and this time the sun and moon and eleven stars were bowing down to me."

¹⁰ When he told his father as well as his brothers, his father rebuked him and said, "What is this dream you had? Will your mother and I and your brothers

actually come and bow down to the ground before you?" **11** His brothers were jealous of him, but his father kept the matter in mind.

Genesis 37:19-20 **19** "Here comes that dreamer!" they said to each other. **20** "Come now, let's kill him and throw him into one of these cisterns and say that a ferocious animal devoured him. Then we'll see what comes of his dreams."

Please read **Genesis 37** in its entirety for complete understanding.

Vision Check: Think about the promises of God as a promotion. When you have a job and your manager tells you that you will be promoted next month, however, you know everyone else wants that position, do you walk out of the office telling all your co-workers? No! You keep it to yourself and allow the manager to make the announcement. Don't be like Joseph, telling all your dreams. Allow God to promote you and announce it.

9 DELAY, NOT DENIAL

Scripture: 2 Peter 3:8 But do not forget this one thing, dear friends: With the Lord, a day is like a thousand years, and a thousand years are like a day. **NIV**

Message: A delay is not a denial.

Natural Eyes: When God speaks to us, we naturally get excited. Why wouldn't we, He is God! He is the one who knows our destiny before we were even formed in our mother's womb. He is the one who can make all things new. The one who gives us new life each day and heals our every pain. He's a miracle performing, promise-keeping, needs providing, God. Knowing this, when God speaks to us and promises us successful businesses, promotions, increase, peace, and joy, we get excited. When it doesn't happen immediately, we get frustrated. The excitement begins to disappear, and doubt appears when you get weary in waiting.

Heavenly Glasses: Revisit the story of Joseph. We left off with him being handed over to Potiphar, Pharaoh's official. **Genesis 39:2-4** talks about how God favored Joseph, and because of that, he found favor with Potiphar. He was allowed to live in the house, and he was placed in charge of the household and everything that Potiphar owned.

God's favor is not limited to circumstances or locations. If you are in a storm, God's favor may look like a child-sized umbrella. You aren't totally blocked from the rainfall, but you also aren't getting as wet as you could. Instead of looking for the rainbow, thank God for what He did provide.

> **God's favor is not limited to circumstances or locations.**

Joseph found favor with Potiphar. He also found unwanted favor with Potiphar's wife. In **Genesis 39:7-10**, she asked him to come to bed with her and he declined. Be wary of those trying to entice you to do unholy things. They cannot be trusted. They see the anointing on your life and are being used by the enemy to destroy you.

Genesis 39:11-20, Potiphar's wife lied and said that Joseph took advantage of her. Potiphar then had Joseph thrown in prison. **Genesis 39:21,** says that the Lord was with Joseph and he found favor with the warden. ***Favor Followed Joseph.***

Joseph had dreams that his brothers would bow down to him and this was the second time that he was thrown into captivity. This was the second time that he was at the mercy of someone else. I have to imagine that Joseph wondered, God, have you forgotten me? Am I no longer worthy of your promises? Have I somehow been disqualified? Or he thought that the blessings reserved for him were transferred over to someone else. But God was **STILL** with him. Even the warden had to favor him because of the God that lives within him.

Amid the delay, God will send reminders that He is not a liar, and you are not denied. For Joseph, the reminders came in the form of continued favor. Regardless of what situation he was placed in, God favored him.

Genesis 40, discusses how Pharaoh had two of his officials, the chief baker, and chief cupbearer, placed in jail and they were under Joseph's care. Both officials had a dream and were looking for someone to interpret them. Joseph provided interpretation for both dreams. He told the chief baker that he would be killed, and he was. He told the chief cupbearer that his dream meant he would be restored to his position with Pharaoh in three days. He asked the chief cupbearer to remember him and tell Pharaoh of him so he could be released. Joseph's interpretation was accurate, but the chief cupbearer forgot Joseph.

Two years later, Pharaoh had dreams and was unable to find anyone to interpret them. At that moment, the cupbearer remembered Joseph. **(Genesis 41)**

Joseph was bought to Pharaoh, and he interpreted his dreams. He told him that there would be seven years of abundance, followed by seven years of famine. Joseph told Pharaoh that he needed to put someone in charge of the land who would store some of the harvests in preparation for the famine. Pharaoh chose Joseph to be in charge. ***Favor followed Joseph.***

After years of punishment, captivity, struggles, stress, and questioning God, Joseph was promoted. Joseph was recognized and Joseph was elevated.

Joseph's interpretation of Pharaoh's dream proved to be true. Famine came and Joseph's brothers were sent to Egypt, where Joseph was, to buy grain so they would survive. When they arrived, they bowed down to Joseph, not knowing it was him. His dream was realized. It may take time, but everything God promised you will be yours if you hold on. Don't give in to doubt, don't give up because of trials. Hold on a while longer.

In **Genesis 37**, Joseph had a dream that he would be above his brothers, and they would bow down to him. In **Genesis 42**, and many years later, it happened. His brothers heard his dream and hated him because of it. They sold him, wanted him dead, lied about what happened, and turned their backs on him, but God was with him. Nothing that his brothers did could stop what God had whispered to Joseph in a dream.

God doesn't move the way we want him to move. Just because He said it, doesn't mean that it will happen right now, but it will happen. You must be patient, stay faithful, and remain true to God because He is remaining true to you. Joseph was delayed, but the promise was never denied.

Prayer

Heavenly Father, I thank you for the delay. I trust that what you said will be and your promises will come to pass. I trust that every dream will come true, every goal will be reached, and every word whispered in the still of the night will see the light of day. I pray for patience as I wait. I pray for the strength to do my part, to spread your word, live your will and do the work as I wait. I pray that my faith doesn't waver. Everything that was set up for my destruction will be used for my good. I pray that victory is my name in this. When they try to blur my vision, I pray you are the clarity. When they try to kill my dreams, I pray you to enlarge my territory. When I question it, God remind me that the delay is never a denial. If you said it, it will be. I thank you even for this. Amid turmoil, confusion, and betrayal, I rejoice even in this. God, I pray, and I wait. I trust you to increase my faith. It shall be, In Jesus' name. Amen.

Chapter 9 Recap

Takeaway: Things in your life will occur at God's appointed time. Don't get weary in waiting, know that a delay is not a denial.

Scripture:

2 Peter 3:8 [8] But do not forget this one thing, dear friends: With the Lord, a day is like a thousand years, and a thousand years are like a day.

Also review, Genesis 39-41.

Vision Check

1. Has God promised you anything?
2. Does it feel like it's taking too long for His promise to manifest?
3. Do you feel like people are trying to kill your dreams?

Just because what God promised you has not happened yet, doesn't mean that it won't. God is not a man that He should lie. His time is not our time; therefore, the wait may be a bit longer than we are comfortable with. The wait may be painful but understand that all things are working for your good.

10 FAVOR AIN'T FAIR

Scripture: Romans 9:15-16 For he says to Moses, "I will have mercy on whom I have mercy, and I will have compassion on whom I have compassion." [16] It does not, therefore, depend on human desire or effort, but on God's mercy. **NIV**

Message: You don't have to do anything spectacular for God to choose you as the recipient of His blessings.

Natural Eyes: You look at your mistakes, social class, bank statement, or family and decide that you are unworthy of greatness. You feel that God will pour down his blessings on you when you are wealthier. You believe that you will get a better job when you get a degree. You have convinced yourself that your business must have more revenue before you get the big investors. You tell yourself all the reasons that you will not be blessed based on the circumstances that you see and that causes you to not look to God. You refuse to turn to Him because you feel He will not acknowledge you in your now.

Heavenly Glasses: We reward our children because of their good behavior, but God isn't like us. Our resources are limited, therefore our rewards to our children are numbered. God has the abundance and is willing to give us an overflow of blessings. He is total power and can do whatever He wants, including bless the unworthy. There are many instances in the Bible where an unlikely person was chosen by God, used by God, and blessed by God.

Elizabeth and her husband, Zachariah, longed for a child. They reached old age and believed that their request was denied because surely, she was too old now. The Lord sent the angel Gabriel to Zachariah and told him that his wife would give him a son. Zachariah was in disbelief. **(Luke 1:5-25)** Zachariah saw natural limits but was dealing with a supernatural God.

I'm sure they had tried for many years to

conceive, and Elizabeth was **told** by all the doctors that she was infertile. It was disgraceful in that time for a woman to be unable to conceive. If we are honest, there is still shame surrounding infertility in today's time. At Elizabeth's age, she had given up on the thought of ever being a mom. BUT GOD! God doesn't have to follow the rules because He makes them. He didn't have to respect that Elizabeth was too old by man's standards, He said that all things are possible.

Elizabeth became pregnant and gave birth to John the Baptist. She was counted out, too old, and disgraced, but God said she was chosen to birth the one who would go before Christ. She was chosen to birth the one who would baptize Jesus. Elizabeth wasn't the healthiest, she wasn't the youngest or most fertile in the land, but she was still chosen.

There were likely some younger women, who were suffering through infertility and felt that it was unfair that Elizabeth was having a child. Why her and not me? That's the thought that filled them up as they saw her belly grow. Envy rose in them because they weren't receiving the same blessing that Elizabeth received. This is evidence that favor ain't fair.

Another notable example is Moses. The Lord came to Moses and told him that he was being sent to Egypt to free His people from Pharaoh. Moses was hesitant, afraid, and felt unworthy. He didn't know how he could complete such a task because he was only a man. He had no power and no authority, so he thought. Moses told God that he could not speak to the people because he was not, "eloquent in speech." God responded that He would help him to speak. When Moses was still hesitant, God told him that he would send his brother, Aaron, with him and He (God) would help them both speak. He would guide them in their words and actions to complete God's will. Moses wasn't chosen because he already possessed the skills, he was given the skills because he was chosen. God desired to use him.

Those are two examples of people who had done nothing spectacular but were still chosen by God. Saul is an example of the opposite. Saul's goal was to destroy the church and murder God's people. While he was on his way to persecute more followers of Christ, Jesus spoke to him. Jesus called him to a greater purpose. Even though he was a murderer and had done everything to be disqualified from the grace of God, he was still chosen. Saul went on to preach because he was chosen despite his past. God grabbed him up in the midst of his wrongdoing and changed his course. God desired him. **(Acts 9)**

That's all that is required, a desire. If God has a desire to use you, rest assured that he has a desire to bless you. We are all qualified in Christ.

Stop focusing on the reasons that you should be overlooked and turn your attention to the one who lives within you. God can do all things; therefore, you can do all things.

Speak to yourself: I am qualified in Him. I can do all things through Christ who strengthens me.

ON THE FLIP SIDE

In understanding that no one can come in between you and the plans of God, you must also understand that God has plans for everyone. There is a promotion with your neighbor's name on it and it would be in your best interest to not allow the spirit of jealousy to creep in. This may be someone else's season to start a successful business, have a new baby, or go on vacation. You lose sight of what God has specifically for you when you focus on what He is giving to others. In the same way that you deserve support and celebration for the wonderful things that God is doing for you, other people deserve that from you.

When you are attached to people who are being blessed, you will still get blessed also. We don't serve a God of just enough, but a God of overflow. This means that He will bless your neighbor in such a large manner that some of those blessings will automatically pour over to you.

Rejoice when God shows up for the people surrounding you. This is an indication that you are in good company and on the right path. Stick close to them and while you reap the benefits of their blessings, take solace in knowing that they will reap the benefits of yours. My pastor says that we serve a God of, "too much, more than enough, overflow." I love that saying because it's a reminder to not limit God's grace, His mercy, and His abundance of rewards for us.

Prayer

Heavenly Father, I pray that you open my eyes to see myself the way that you see me. Thank you for blessing me despite me. Thank you for changing the requirements when my qualifications didn't match up. Thank you for placing something in me that shines through to the world. God, I thank you for placing people in my life who are being blessed. Continue to touch my friends and my family in a mighty way. Remove any jealousy from me and allow me only to rejoice when you work. Thank you for being a good, good God and loving me through everything. Amen

Chapter 10 Recap

Takeaway: You are qualified in God.

Scriptures:

Romans 9:15-16 For he says to Moses, "I will have mercy on whom I have mercy, and I will have compassion on whom I have compassion." **16** It does not, therefore, depend on human desire or effort, but on God's mercy.

Luke 1:13 But the angel said to him: "Do not be afraid, Zechariah; your prayer has been heard. Your wife Elizabeth will bear you a son, and you are to call him John.

Luke 1:23-25 **23** When his time of service was completed, he returned home. **24** After this his wife Elizabeth became pregnant and for five months remained in seclusion. **25** "The Lord has done this for me," she said. "In these days he has shown his favor and taken away my disgrace among the people."

Please review Acts 9 to read about Saul

Vision Check:

Think back on the mistakes you have made. Reflect on ways that you have not honored God or done what you know you should have. Now, blow on your hand. Breath in your body is proof that God is still blessing you in spite of any of your wrongdoings.

11 CRACKS IN YOUR CIRCLE

Scripture: **Mark 4:39** He got up, rebuked the wind, and said to the waves, "Quiet! Be still!" Then the wind died down and it was completely calm.

Message: Pay attention to the company that you keep.

Natural Eyes: We've been friends for 20 years; I can't turn my back on them now. I know he's hurting me, but he has a good heart. Mama has been using me and lying to me, but she's my mother, I can't cut her off. Everyone knows how they are; they are set in their ways. We're family, we have longevity, I don't want to start over. I don't want to be alone, I'm afraid of the unknown. I am comfortable.

Heavenly Glasses: Guard who you allow in your life and remove anyone who means you no good. It sounds like a simple concept, so why wouldn't everyone do this? I'll tell you why. ***Emotions***. We fall in love with someone, and we become blinded by our emotions. We see that we aren't thriving in life, and we blame everything EXCEPT our connections. We blame everyone EXCEPT ourselves for being tied to someone who God does not want to prosper from our blessings.

People remain in unhealthy relationships out of obligation, comfort, or fear. Whether it's your relative, friend, coworker, or acquaintance, there is no reason to keep people in your life if they are causing more harm than good.

> **There is no reason to keep people in your life if they are causing more harm than good.**

When emotional ties are removed, and you focus on what this person contributes or takes away from your life, you can see if they are the cause or cure for the storm.

Imagine being on a boat and you have your friends/crew on the boat. The boat starts to shake, and you begin to sink. You need to identify where the winds are coming from. Why did the storm begin? Is there someone on your boat that caused the storm? Did your actions cause the storm?

When evaluating who is on your boat there are three distinct types of people that I want you to keep in mind. Some people contribute, and you will benefit from their presence. Then there are the people who will block your blessings because they do not belong in your life, and you have the people who are just there and taking up space. Take a moment and look around. What type of people are you surrounded by? Are they causing you to sink? Do they have power?

The Bible gives the greatest examples of two of these people. First, in the story of Jonah, we see the person who is the cause of the storm. They have the power to calm it, but only by removing themselves from your life.

In studying Jonah **1**, you will see how Jonah was on the boat with the sailors and they had a destination for which they were bound. Jonah was running from his God-given assignment. The winds came, the boat was rocking, items were flying, and people were screaming. The sailors questioned how to stop the storm. They were in distress and only Jonah held the power to stop the winds. The winds came because Jonah was on the boat, so the solution was to remove him. Jonah told the sailors to throw him into the raging sea. Once they threw him in, the winds calmed.

Because he was on their boat, they experienced fear, and their destiny was threatened. God wouldn't allow them to make it to their destination peacefully if Jonah were traveling with them. Jonah wasn't a bad person; he just couldn't go where they were going. Just because people can't go with you, doesn't mean they are bad. You can love these people but love them from a distance. You must be ok with doing what is best for you. Just as someone else's blessings can pour over into us, so can their punishments.

Then we have the person who has been placed in your life with purpose and the power to calm your storms. This person's assignment is tied to yours and they were given to you by God.

Mark 4:35-41, Jesus was on the boat with his disciples and the wind came. I can imagine the fear that set in because something was occurring that was out of their control. They went to Jesus with their fear, and he commanded the wind to stop. He used his power to bring calm to a tumultuous situation. He contributed to their success, and he helped them get to their destination. Jesus was an asset on the boat.

The third type of person is taking up space. They aren't contributing anything great or causing any storms, but they still can be blocking your blessings. Be careful with these people. Although they may not be hurting you, the space that they are taking could be filled with God's blessings. Would you pour into a full cup?

How do you know who is who? You must stay in prayer and ask God for the spirit of discernment. You don't want to remove the wrong people or keep the wrong people around. Most importantly, you need to reevaluate your circle. You are well within your spiritual rights to take inventory and remove people.

Prayer

God, I pray for the spirit of discernment. Reveal to me who should stay and who should go. Give me the strength to release toxic people and the will to hold close the ones who add value. Open my eyes to see people for who they are and what they do. If I move too slow, remove them for me. When you remove them, give me peace in their departure. Surround me with the strong, powerful, godly people who have a purpose in my life. Knowing that you can and will do exactly what I have asked, I thank you. In Jesus' name, Amen.

Chapter 11 Recap

Takeaway: Everyone in your life serves a purpose. They either lift you or pull you down.

Scripture:

Mark 4:35-41 [35] That day when evening came, he said to his disciples, "Let us go over to the other side." [36] Leaving the crowd behind, they took him along, just as he was, in the boat. There were also other boats with him. [37] A furious squall came up, and the waves broke over the boat so that it was nearly swamped. [38] Jesus was in the stern, sleeping on a cushion. The disciples woke him and said to him, "Teacher, don't you care if we drown?"

[39] He got up, rebuked the wind, and said to the waves, "Quiet! Be still!" Then the wind died down and it was completely calm.

[40] He said to his disciples, "Why are you so afraid? Do you still have no faith?"

[41] They were terrified and asked each other, "Who is this? Even the wind and the waves obey him!"

Please review Jonah

Vision Check: Take inventory

- Do you feel drained or energized after interactions?

- Do people call to check on you or only to pull from you?

- Are you satisfied with your circle?

If people are pulling from you and giving nothing back, you must let go.

12 ENTERTAINING ANGELS

Scripture: James 2:1 My brothers and sisters, believers in our glorious Lord Jesus Christ must not show favoritism.

Message: Kindness costs you nothing but could gain you everything.

Natural Eyes: Sometimes, we forget that all people are human. We also forget that all people are God's children and deserve to be treated with respect. We see a homeless person on the street and turn our noses up at them. When they come towards us, we grab our purse, hold our heads down to avoid eye contact, and when they speak to us, we act like we don't hear them. Without saying it, we think that we are better than the people around us.

The janitor doesn't get treated with the same respect as the CEO. We walk past people on the street without acknowledging them. We get caught up in ourselves and forget to respect and learn from the people around us.

Heavenly Glasses: I remember working at a job and at the end of our training, we received a small bronze trophy of a janitor. When the gift was explained, they told us that every person in the company was as valuable as the next. They gave the trophy of the janitor to remind us that even in our positions, we are not above or beneath a person who people frequently think less of. Without the janitor, we could face hazardous situations that could prevent us from doing our jobs, so we must appreciate and respect each person and their role.

When interacting with others, you can never be sure who they are, or more importantly, who they are in Christ. **Genesis 19** talks about two angels who arrived in Sodom. They were greeted by Lot, who did not know that they were angels, and he made an offer for them to stay in his home. Unbeknownst to Lot, they were on a mission to destroy the town. Even without having that knowledge, he fed them and when men came to hurt them, he protected them.

The angels were grateful to Lot for his kindness, the refuge he provided, and his hospitality. Because of this, they told him to get his family and leave the town because God sent them to destroy it. Lot found favor because he showed kindness and respect without knowing he had been entertaining angels.

The beggar on the street could be a test. God may want to see your grace before He extends His. Don't ever think that you are more worthy than the next person or too important to show kindness. Remember that God does not show favoritism, He loves us all on an equal level. Therefore, you should treat all people equally.

> **God may want to see your grace before He extends His.**

Prayer

God, I pray for the wisdom to treat all people the same. If I ever get boastful, if I ever get arrogant and forget that we are all children of the most high, I pray you gently bring your teachings to my remembrance. Teach me to be humble and ensure my actions line up with your word and teachings. If anyone has been hurt by my actions or my words, or if I have sinned in my thoughts, I pray for forgiveness. I pray that the same love that you give to me, I am capable of giving to others. I thank you in advance. In Jesus' name, Amen.

CHAPTER 12 RECAP

Takeaway: Treat people the way that you want to be treated.

Scriptures:

James 2:1-7 My brothers and sisters, believers in our glorious Lord Jesus Christ must not show favoritism. [2] Suppose a man comes into your meeting wearing a gold ring and fine clothes, and a poor man in filthy old clothes also comes in. [3] If you show special attention to the man wearing fine clothes and say, "Here's a good seat for you," but say to the poor man, "You stand there" or "Sit on the floor by my feet," [4] have you not discriminated among yourselves and become judges with evil thoughts?

[5] Listen, my dear brothers and sisters: Has not God chosen those who are poor in the eyes of the world to be rich in faith and to inherit the kingdom he promised those who love him? [6] But you have dishonored the poor. Is it not the rich who are exploiting you? Are they not the ones who are dragging you into court? [7] Are they not the ones who are blaspheming the noble name of him to whom you belong?

Vision Check:

Have you ignored someone because of their status? Have you respected everyone that you have encountered? Have there been times when you have turned your nose up at someone or looked down on them due to their circumstances? How about their education? What about the car they drive, the house they live in, or their marital status? It happens so quickly that we don't realize how we are treating the people that we consider less than us. Take the extra time to be with people and show them that they matter, and they are important. You never know, you could be entertaining angels.

13 THE BOOK OF JOB

The Book of Job

The book of Job is one of my all-time favorite Bible stories. This is what gets me through my darkest hours and most confusing moments. In my life, I have experienced things that made me want to end my life, then I remembered Job. Each time I study Job's struggle, God reveals something new to me. He takes me deeper in understanding pain and sacrifice. This also takes me deeper in understanding God's love and protection in the midst of hurt.

Who Is Job?

Job 1:1-5 establishes Job's character, family, and faith. These five things below are what were important enough to be shared at the beginning of the chapter.

- **Job was a man (Job 1:1)**
- **Job was a good man. (Job 1:1)**
- **Job was a blessed man. (Job 1:2-3)**
- **Job was an important man. (Job 1:3)**
- **Job was a praying man. (Job 1:5)**

Why Job?

We need to first understand that Job was chosen for his hardships. Satan had been traveling the earth and when he reached God, God spoke. God said, "Have you considered my servant Job?" At this moment, God had chosen Job to prove that man's love for God was not dependent on what God gave to man. God chose Job to prove that it was unconditional love between God and His creation.

But why did God choose Job? The Bible says that God told Satan, "...There is no one on earth like him; he is blameless and upright, a man who fears

God and shuns evil." **(Job 1:5)**

With those characteristics, you would think that Job would be rewarded and not punished. In this season, you must understand that the very thing that qualified you for your blessing has qualified you for your test. Don't get weary, do not faint, rest assured that those same characteristics are what guarantee your success.

> *In this season, you must understand that the very thing that qualified you for your blessing has qualified you for your test.*

After God suggested Job, Satan said that Job only worships and praises God because of the blessings he received. He said that if God took away Job's "things," he would surely curse God. **(Job 1:9-11)**

God then gave Satan permission to control or destroy everything that Job had but would not allow him to touch the man. **(Job 1:12)**

> *God places limitations on your trials but there are no limits to your blessings.*

What Happened to Job?

In one day, Job lost his oxen, donkeys, servants, sheep, camels, and all ten of his children. **(Job 1:13-19)** Can you imagine receiving report after report of the things that have been taken away from you suddenly? Try to put yourself in Job's shoes. You're at work and get fired. When you walk out of the job, you find that your car has been repossessed. You catch the bus home to find that your house has burned down with all your belongings inside. Before you can call anyone to assist you, you get a call that your only child was killed. Then your phone gets cut off after that call. I'm talking about losing everything in one day. This is what happened to Job.

Job maintained his love for God and his faith in God. The enemy still wasn't satisfied. When he went back to God, he said that surely Job would curse God if his body was afflicted. At that point, God allowed Satan to afflict Job's body but said he could not take his life. Again, limitations to your suffering. Limitations to your trials and limitations to your hardships will always be present.

Satan afflicted Job's body with painful sores all over. **(Job 2:7)** Job still did not sin against God.

Natural Eyes Vs. Heavenly Glasses

Job had a choice. He could curse God and see the pain in the natural, or he could equip himself with his Heavenly Glasses. When Job lost everything, his response was, **Job 1:21** "…Naked I came from my mother's womb, and naked I will depart. The Lord gave and the Lord has taken away; may the name of the Lord be praised."

When Job's body was afflicted, he could have cursed God, but the Bible says he didn't. When Job's wife (his helpmate, partner, confidant, and friend), told him to curse God, he did not. The Bible says in **Job 2:10**, "He replied, "You are talking like a foolish woman. Shall we accept good from God, and not trouble?" In all this, Job did not sin in what he said."

Job did have his moments where he experienced pain and had natural emotions. He cried out to God, asking why He afflicted him. He cursed the day he was born. He felt defeated and wanted to give up. His natural was strong, but the spirit was stronger. Job had friends who traveled when they heard of his troubles. They traveled to comfort him and told him that he must have sinned against God because that is the only reason that he would be punished so harshly. Some people don't understand your life and will be willing to accuse you of things that are not true. Don't let them convince you that wrong is right and right is wrong. Job knew he had lived an upright life, and just didn't understand why he was suffering

In your trials, believe that God chose you. There is nothing that can occur that God doesn't allow. If He is allowing you to go through things, it's because he knows you are strong enough to continue praising Him. Don't give up in the middle. If you keep pushing towards the end, you will reap the benefits. It's natural for you to get discouraged, read Job and you will see that he got discouraged. But when God speaks, you better open your ears, mind, and heart to Him. Know that you just have to get through some things to get to some better things.

What Comes After the Suffering?

Job 42:10 After Job had prayed for his friends, the Lord restored his fortunes and gave him twice as much as he had before.

Job's blessings in the latter part of his life, exceeded those in the former. He kept living through the bad. He didn't turn away from God. When you are being attacked from every side, remember Job. Job did nothing to deserve the struggle he endured, but he was qualified because God trusted him. Instead of thinking of it as punishment, believe that God said, "Have you considered my good and faithful servant, (**insert name here**)?" You can handle this!

14 DEAR CHILDREN

Scripture: Matthew 19:14 Jesus said, "Let the little children come to me, and do not hinder them, for the kingdom of heaven belongs to such as these."

In life, you will face challenging times and sadness, but that isn't a reason to give up. Things may happen that you don't understand, and frustration may try to make its way into your mind and heart, but you have heavenly glasses that you can put on to view your situations differently.

Remember that as Christians, we believe that the Bible is God's rules for how we should live AND proof of His love towards us. Because we believe in the Bible, we pull our strength from it to live better lives.

The Bible tells us that all things work together for the good of those who love the Lord. (**Romans 8:28**) This means that if anything happens that you think is bad or upsets you, God will turn it into something good for you. If you ever feel that you are missing something or lose a prize, believe that God has something better for you. God is always and forever looking out for you and making sure that you are ok. God wants to teach you a lesson through your experience. When you learn your lesson, you now can help your friend and attempt to prevent them from going through the same tests.

That process may hurt sometimes, but it is still for your good. Diamonds are one of the most precious stones. Do you know how diamonds are made? Placing carbon under intense pressure is key in creating diamonds. It requires pressure. It requires pain. Sometimes things must hurt before you can see the beauty in them.

When you are waiting for something to happen, you may feel like it will never happen, but you need to be patient. It will happen when it is supposed to, not before or after.

Study the instructions in the Bible for a long and prosperous life. Be kind to others. Honor your parents, keep God's commandments, and more than anything else, LOVE.

Keep yourself surrounded by people who love God and will guide you in His way. Don't allow anyone to tell you that you are not valuable to God, because the Bible clearly states that you are. Talk to God. Pray to Him. Thank Him daily and remember that you are special. You are chosen for greatness. You will always win.

Prayer

Heavenly Father, I thank you for my life and pray that you guide me on the right path. Keep me focused on you even when it is easy to be distracted. Please keep me safe from all hurt, harm, and danger that tries to come my way. Forgive me for anything that I have done that is unlike you. I love you. Amen.

Vision Check

I challenge you to pause when faced with difficulties. Pause and remember that all things work together for the good of those who love God. Do you love God? If the answer is yes, know that this is working for your good. Every encounter you have can be a heavenly experience if you look at it through your heavenly glasses. God is always working on our behalf and His blessings, grace, and mercy are always available for His children.

Prayer

God, I pray for me. I pray that you open my heart to your word, your will, and your way. Give me strength in my weakness and peace in my discomfort. Give me joy in my place of sadness and trade my brokenness for your healing. Restore my health when I am faced with sickness. Allow your shield of protection to surround me when the enemy wants to claim my life. Increase my faith when it begins to waver. God, I love you and just want to live a life pleasing to you. Guide me, Lord. Keep me, Lord. Now I thank you in advance for all that I know you will do. I thank you for being Lord over my life and my circumstances. I rest knowing that you will do just what your word said you would do. I thank you now, for tomorrow. I trust you now for the future. In Jesus' name, Amen.

Ebony Collins is an award-winning author, Licensed Life Coach Minister, mother, and wife. Her mission is to encourage God's people and show them, genuine love, while inspiring them to pursue their goals.

www.ingramcontent.com/pod-product-compliance
Lightning Source LLC
Chambersburg PA
CBHW072157160426
43197CB00012B/2427